I'm Going to ITALY
Activity Journal

From the Author of Learn About Italy for Kids

IBSN 978-1-0689039-1-5

What's in This Book

Journal

The book includes 60 daily journal pages. 30 are filled with prompts, and 30 are blank for doing whatever you want (e.g., drawing a picture, taping in a souvenir, or writing more because you have a lot to say).

There are some slight differences in the prompts, so flip through and complete whichever one suits the day you just had. For example, if you laughed a lot on a particular day, fill in the page with the prompt "What made me laugh?". It's okay if the journal pages are out of order; you can even miss days. Or you can complete as many pages as you want on a day full of adventures you don't want to forget. Just put the correct date on the top of the page, and away you go!

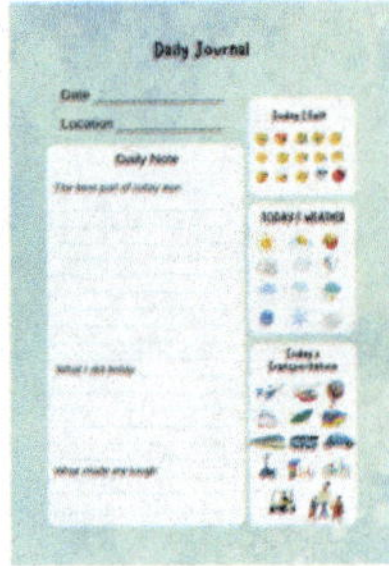

Puzzles, Games and Mazes

There are fun Italy-themed games throughout the book. They are placed in different spots that make sense for your trip. For example, there's an Airport/Train Station Bingo game at the front of the book and another at the back. These will help you fill the times you must wait around for sometimes hours at a time.

Where a puzzle has a specific answer, like a maze, you'll find these at the back of the book.

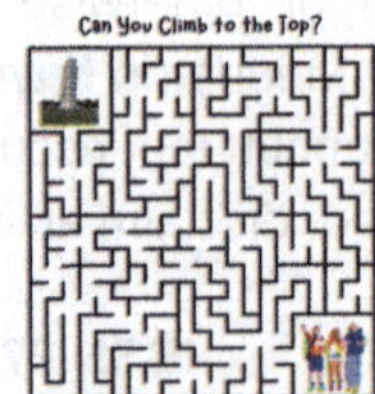

Templates, Tips & Facts

We included some handy tips, like packing your suitcase and carry-on and preventing jet lag. Although an adult is likely to pack for you, it's helpful to understand these tips to be more independent when you travel. Soon, you'll become an experienced globetrotter!

Italy is a fantastic country, and there is so much to experience. So, we added a few facts throughout the book to help you better understand what you might see.

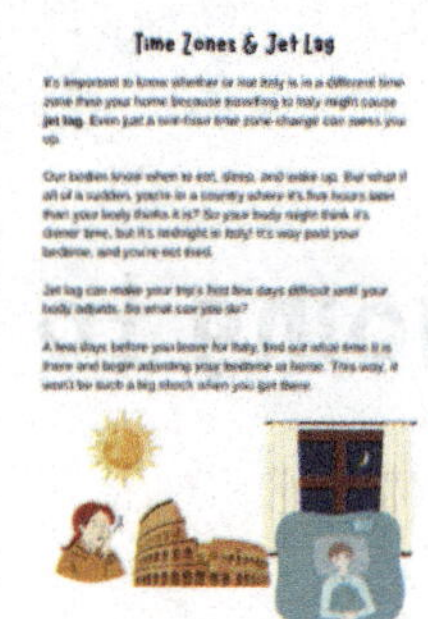

Buon viaggio in Italia!

Have a good trip in Italy!

This book belongs to:

Name _________________________   Age________

I'm going to Italy!

Date we leave: ________________________________

Date we come home: ________________________

Who's coming with me: ______________________

____

____

How Far Will You Travel?

Can you find your country on this map? Colour it in, then draw an arrow to Italy (that's the blue country in the middle of the map).

Next, circle how you will get there.

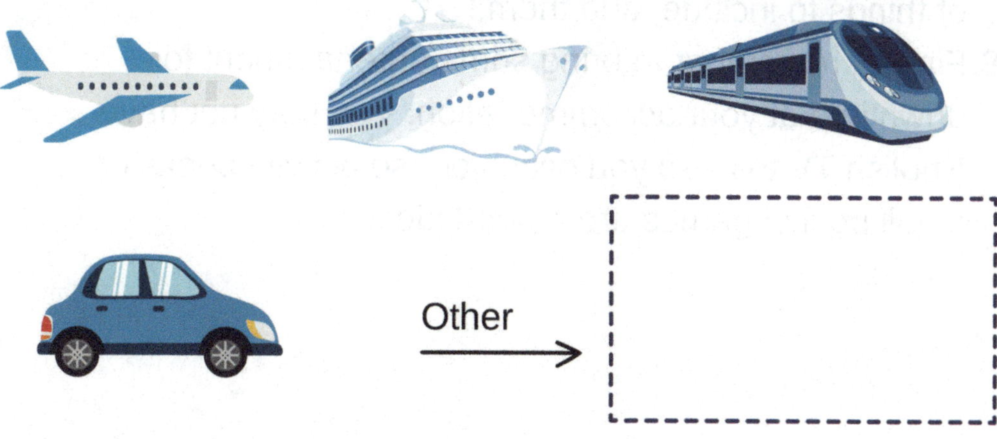

Tips for Packing Your Suitcase For a Flight

1. Keep a packing list.
2. Don't overpack - leave room for souvenirs.
3. Stick to a color theme for your clothes to mix and match your outfits.
4. Even if where you're going is warm, always pack a sweater or jacket.
5. Pack little things inside of big things. For example, pack some socks inside your hat.
6. Place something outside your suitcase to immediately recognize it on the airport carousel. For example, tie a short ribbon of your favorite colour to the handle.
7. Don't wait until the last minute. Begin packing a few days before you leave with your checklist nearby. As you think of things to include, add them.
8. Finally, remember to bring some entertainment for downtime at your accommodation. You may not have English TV to keep you occupied, so activity books or small pocket games are a good idea.

Suitcase Packing List

Tips for Packing Your Carry-on For a Flight

1. Your backpack is an ideal carry-on.
2. Any liquids must be 3.4 ounces or 100 millilitres or smaller per item. If they are bigger (for example, sunscreen), they need to go in your suitcase.
3. Then, your liquids need to go into one plastic bag so it can be inspected by airport security.
4. Pack a reusable water bottle. Once you pass through security, you can fill it with water for the flight.
5. Pack one complete change of clothes into your carry-on in case your suitcase is delayed in Italy.
6. Include something to entertain you in the airport and on the plane, for example, an activity book and markers, puzzle games, or something to read. Don't forget to pack this book! 😉
7. Add a snack (nothing messy) to enjoy while you wait in the airport.
8. Put a little note in one of the outside pockets, including your first name and the phone number of an adult travelling with you. If you accidentally leave your carry-on behind somewhere, someone can call and arrange to return it to you.

Carry-on Packing List

Time Zones & Jet Lag

It's important to know whether or not Italy is in a different time zone than your home because travelling to Italy might cause **jet lag.** Even just a one-hour time zone change can mess you up.

Our bodies know when to eat, sleep, and wake up. But what if all of a sudden, you're in a country where it's five hours later than your body thinks it is? So your body might think it's dinner time, but it's midnight in Italy! It's way past your bedtime, and you're not tired.

Jet lag can make your trip's first few days difficult until your body adjusts. So what can you do?

A few days before you leave for Italy, find out what time it is there and begin adjusting your bedtime at home. This way, it won't be such a big shock when you get there.

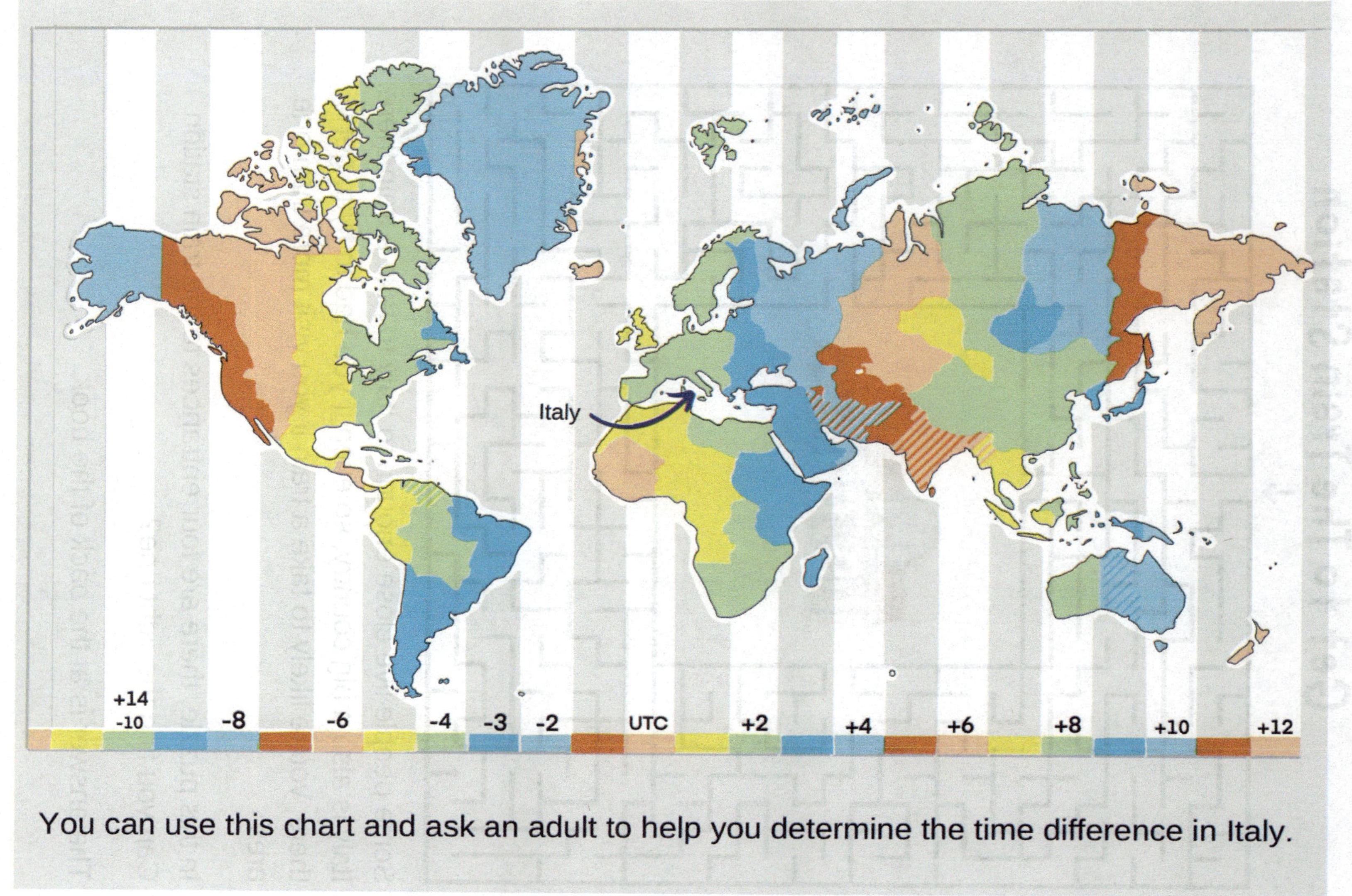

You can use this chart and ask an adult to help you determine the time difference in Italy.

Get to The Train Station

Some people live close enough to Italy to take a train there. Italy is also a big country, so even if you had to fly to get there, you're likely to take a train if you visit more than one area.

In this puzzle, there are four entrances to the train station. Can you find the right one?

The answer is at the back of the book.

Airport/Train Station Bingo

Whether you're flying or taking a train, you'll have to wait around a lot. So here's a great chance for a game of bingo!

Just X out everything you see. Can you get a straight line? How about a full card?

A different bingo card is at the back of the book for your return trip from Italy.

Daily Journal – Travel Day

Date ________________________

Location ______________________

Daily Note

The best part of today was:

What I saw today:

Today was exhausting because:

Today I Felt

TODAY'S WEATHER

Today's Transportation

A Picture is Worth a Thousand Words

Draw, write or doodle in this space to represent your day

Daily Journal

Date ______________________

Location ______________________

Daily Note

The best part of today was:

What I did today:

I was excited to see:

Today I Felt

TODAY'S WEATHER

Today's Transportation

A Picture is Worth a Thousand Words

Draw, write or doodle in this space to represent your day

Daily Journal

Date _______________________

Location _______________________

Daily Note

The best part of today was:

What I did today:

What made me laugh:

Today I Felt

TODAY'S WEATHER

Today's Transportation

A Picture is Worth a Thousand Words

Draw, write or doodle in this space to represent your day

Italian Food

The food in Italy is delicious! Even if you eat gluten-free or dairy-free, most Italian restaurants (especially in tourist areas) provide options. So if you want to try Italian pasta or pizza, you can order a gluten or dairy-free version.

Here are some popular dishes in Italy that you might want to try. And to make it even more fun, you can complete the Food Bingo throughout your trip. See how many new and delicious dishes you're willing to try.

Risotto - creamy rice dish with broth and sometimes seafood
Pizza - Italian flatbread with tomato sauce, cheese and other toppings
Pasta - types of noodles traditionally served with sauce
Gnocchi - soft dough dumplings made from potatoes, flour and eggs
Pesto alla Genovese - sauce made from herbs, parmesan & olive oil
Lasagne - layered pasta dish with meat, cream sauce and cheese
Gelato - Italian-style ice cream
Tiramisu - coffee-soaked biscuits with mascarpone cheese and cocoa
Carbonara - pasta dish made with eggs, cheese and pancetta (pork)
Ossobuco - braised veal cooked with wine, broth and vegetables
Bruschetta - toasted bread topped with garlic, tomatoes and olive oil
Prosciutto di Parma - thinly sliced cured ham appetizer
Parmigiano Reggiano - hard cheese often grated over dishes
Burrata - creamy Italian cheese made from mozzarella and cream
Focaccia di Recco col Formaggio - thin crisp bread filled with cheese
Arancini - deep-fried rice balls filled with ragu, mozzarella and peas
Polenta - boiled cornmeal, can be served creamy or fried
Minestrone - vegetable soup with beans, pasta or rice
Caprese Salad - sliced mozzarella, tomatoes, basil and olive oil
Ribollita - soup made with bread, beans and vegetables
Spaghetti alle Vongole - pasta with clams, garlic, olive oil and wine
Fiorentina Steak - steak from Chianina cattle, grilled and served rare
Vitello Tonnato - cold veal slices topped with a creamy tuna sauce
Agnolotti - stuffed pasta filled with meat or vegetables
Cannoli - crispy pastry shell filled with sweet ricotta cheese

Buon Appetito!

Italian Food Bingo

Are you an adventurous foodie? One of the best things about travel is trying new and sometimes exotic foods. Cross off each item you ate or at least tasted while in Italy. Can you get a straight line? How about the whole card?

How Did You Score?

no lines = are you a picky eater?
1 line = nice try
2 lines = good job
3 lines - impressive
4 lines = you are a brave soul
full card = you are a foodie extraordinaire!

Daily Journal

Date _______________________

Location _______________________

Daily Note

The best part of today was:

What I did today:

Today I tried _______________________

for the first time.

It was _______________________.

Today I Felt

TODAY'S WEATHER

Today's Transportation

A Picture is Worth a Thousand Words

Draw, write or doodle in this space to represent your day

Daily Journal

Date ________________________

Location ________________________

Daily Note

The best part of today was:

What we did today:

Where we went:

Today I Felt

TODAY'S WEATHER

Today's Transportation

A Picture is Worth a Thousand Words

Draw, write or doodle in this space to represent your day

Daily Journal

Date _______________________

Location _______________________

Daily Note

The best part of today was:

What I did today:

What I ate:

Was it good?

Today I Felt

TODAY'S WEATHER

Today's Transportation

A Picture is Worth a Thousand Words

Draw, write or doodle in this space to represent your day

Italian Things Sudoku (easy)

draw the correct shape in each square so that each picture appears only once in a column and once in a row.

The solution is at the back of the book.

flag

pizza

gondola

Leaning Tower of Pisa

olive

I Spy

Daily Journal

Date _______________________

Location _______________________

Daily Note

The best part of today was:

What I did today:

Well this was an unexpected surprise:

Today I Felt

TODAY'S WEATHER

Today's Transportation

A Picture is Worth a Thousand Words

Draw, write or doodle in this space to represent your day

Daily Journal

Date _______________________

Location _______________________

Daily Note

The best part of today was:

What I did today:

What made today challenging:

Today I Felt

TODAY'S WEATHER

Today's Transportation

A Picture is Worth a Thousand Words

Draw, write or doodle in this space to represent your day

Daily Journal

Date ___________________________

Location ___________________________

Daily Note

The best part of today was:

What I did today:

What made me laugh:

Today I Felt

TODAY'S WEATHER

Today's Transportation

A Picture is Worth a Thousand Words

Draw, write or doodle in this space to represent your day

Rome Colosseum
The Colosseum could hold up to 50,000 people, making it one of the largest amphitheaters ever built
It took 10 years to build and they used over a million tons of stone, concrete and bricks.
There is a series of underground tunnels called the hypogeum. It's where gladiators and fighting animals waited until their turn to go into the arena to fight.

Use the hypogeum to get to the arena

Venationes were Roman games in which men fought wild animals, including lions, tigers, crocodiles, and bears. Imagine you're the gladiator. Can you find your way through the tunnels and get to the lion?

The solution to the puzzle is at the back of the book.

Daily Journal

Date ___________________

Location ________________

Today I Felt

Daily Note

The best part of today was:

What I did today:

I was fascinated to learn that:

TODAY'S WEATHER

Today's Transportation

A Picture is Worth a Thousand Words

Draw, write or doodle in this space to represent your day

Daily Journal

Date _______________________

Location _________________

Daily Note

The best part of today was:

What I did today:

Today I Felt

TODAY'S WEATHER

Today's Transportation

A Picture is Worth a Thousand Words

Draw, write or doodle in this space to represent your day

Daily Journal

Date ___________________________

Location ___________________________

Daily Note

The best part of today was:

What I did today:

Today I Felt

TODAY'S WEATHER

Today's Transportation

A Picture is Worth a Thousand Words

Draw, write or doodle in this space to represent your day

The Leaning Tower of Pisa

The Tower is 56 meters tall (183.7 feet), and there are 294 steps to reach the top. For the price of a ticket, you can climb the tower as long as you are at least 8 years old, and you are with an adult.

The Leaning Tower of Pisa was built in the 12th century and began to lean from day one. The reason it leans is because of the soft and unstable ground it was built on.

Can You Climb to the Top?

Warning: The marble steps can be uneven and slippery. The winding staircase and the building's lean can make you dizzy. And it can get very hot and stuffy inside, especially on a hot day.

Now that you have proper shoes and your water bottle with you, do you think you can climb all 294 steps to the top?

The solution to the maze is at the back of the book.

Daily Journal

Date _______________________

Location _______________________

Daily Note

The best part of today was:

What I did today:

Today I tried _______________

for the very first time. And it was:

Today I Felt

TODAY'S WEATHER

Today's Transportation

A Picture is Worth a Thousand Words

Draw, write or doodle in this space to represent your day

Daily Journal

Date ___________________

Location ___________________

Daily Note

The best part of today was:

What I did today:

Today I Felt

TODAY'S WEATHER

Today's Transportation

A Picture is Worth a Thousand Words

Draw, write or doodle in this space to represent your day

Daily Journal

Date _____________________

Location _____________________

Daily Note

The best part of today was:

What I did today:

Today I learned:

Today I Felt

TODAY'S WEATHER

Today's Transportation

A Picture is Worth a Thousand Words

Draw, write or doodle in this space to represent your day

Sample Logic Puzzle

Find out which boy is which age, and what month is each boy's birthday.

	Jake	Joe	Tim	Eric	8	9	10	11
April								
May								
June								
July								
8				
9				
10				
11				

clues
1. Jake was born in July
2. Joe is 11
3. The 9 year old was born in April
4. The person born in May is 8
5. Tim's birthday is in May
6. The person born in July is 10

How to Complete This Sample Puzzle

So, let's take each clue and place check marks where we know the answer. See the grid #1

Next, we'll place an X to eliminate the other options. For example, if we know Joe is 11, we also know he is NOT 8, 9 or 10. And we know that neither Jake, Tim, nor Eric are 11, so we also eliminate those. See grid #2.

Continue by looking at each of the 6 clues until there are 2 checks in each column and two checks in each row.

column ↕   row ↔

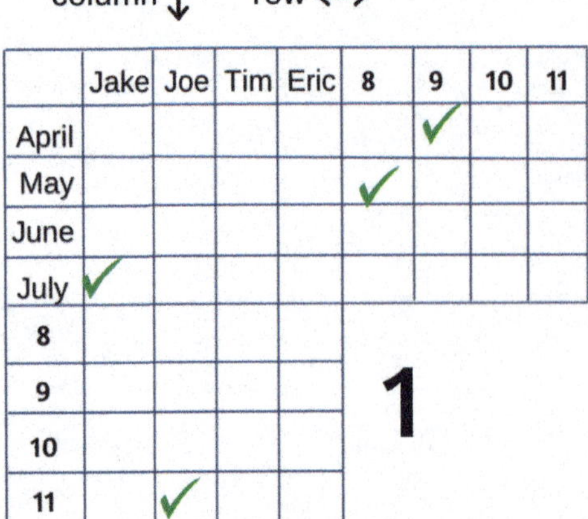

Italian Vacation - Logic Puzzle (hard)

Four families (Adams, Chong, Garcia, and Jones) vacationed in Italy. Each family went to either Rome, Venice, Naples, or Pisa. The vacations lasted 7, 10, 14, or 21 days. Use the clues below to determine where and how long each family vacationed.

	Rome	Venice	Naples	Pisa	7 days	10 days	14 days	21 days
Adams								
Chong								
Garcia								
Jones								
7 days								
10 days								
14 days								
21 days								

When you know something for sure, place a check in the box. Then place X's in the other boxes for that row and column.

The solution is at the back of the book.

Clues:

1. The Adams were on vacation twice as long as the family who went to Pisa.
2. The family that was gone for 21 days visited Naples.
3. The Jones family visited the city that invented pizza.
4. The Garcia family went to the city of canals for more than a week.
5. The Chong family went to Pisa to take a funny photo.
6. The Adams family vacationed in the capital of Italy.

Daily Journal

Date _______________________

Location _______________________

Daily Note

The best part of today was:

What I did today:

Today was:

Busy ☐   Chill ☐

Today I Felt

TODAY'S WEATHER

Today's Transportation

A Picture is Worth a Thousand Words

Draw, write or doodle in this space to represent your day

Daily Journal

Date _______________________

Location _______________________

Daily Note

The best part of today was:

What I did today:

What surprised me most:

Today I Felt

TODAY'S WEATHER

Today's Transportation

A Picture is Worth a Thousand Words

Draw, write or doodle in this space to represent your day

Daily Journal

Date _______________________

Location _______________________

Daily Note

The best part of today was:

What I did today:

Today I got to try:

Today I Felt

TODAY'S WEATHER

Today's Transportation

A Picture is Worth a Thousand Words

Draw, write or doodle in this space to represent your day

Italian Things Sudoku (medium)

Fill in the squares by drawing the shape to ensure each picture appears only once in a column and once in a row.

The solution is at the back of the book.

pizza

flag

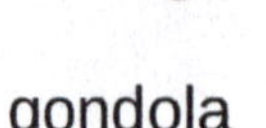
gondola

Pisa

olive

gladiator

Italian Things Sudoku (hard)

Fill in the squares by drawing the shape to ensure each picture appears only once in a column and once in a row. **There is an added challenge:** Each sub-section of 9 squares must also have no repeats.

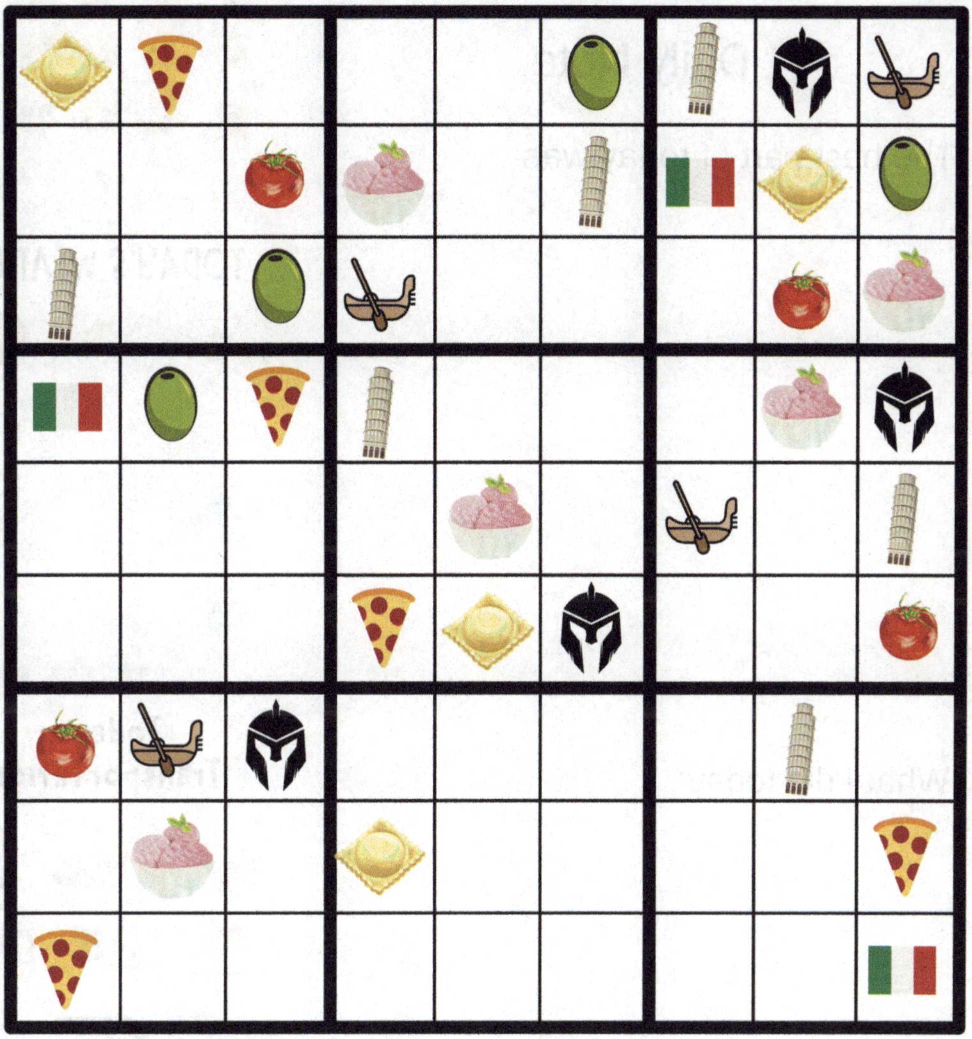

The solution is at the back of the book.

 pizza  flag  gondola  Pisa  olive  gladiator  tomato  gelato  ravioli

Daily Journal

Date ______________________

Location __________________

Daily Note

The best part of today was:

What I did today:

Today I Felt

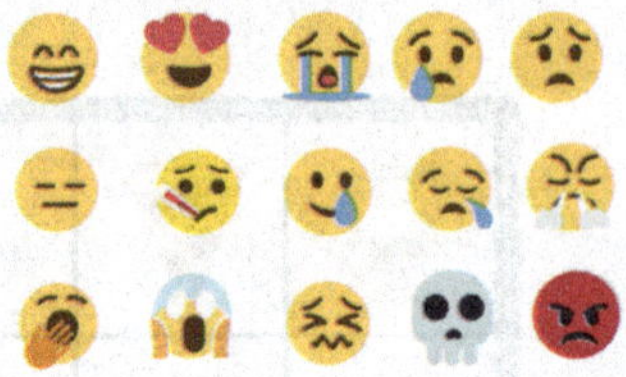

TODAY'S WEATHER

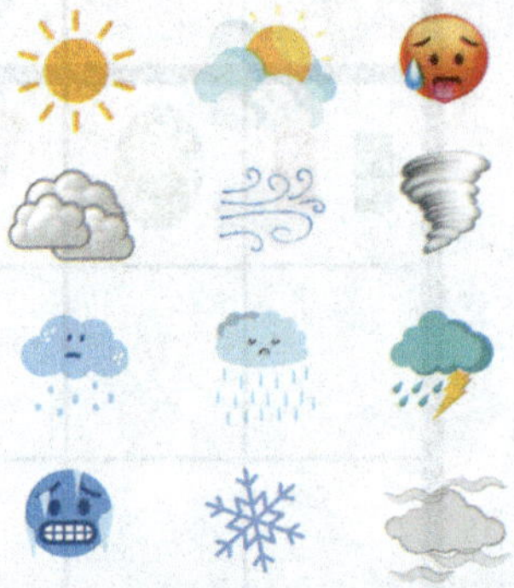

Today's Transportation

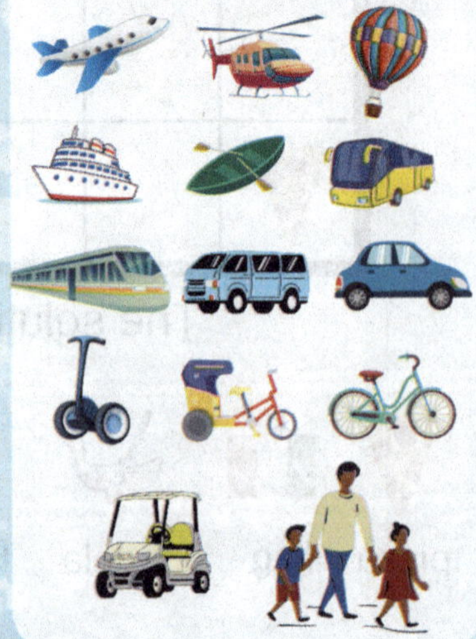

A Picture is Worth a Thousand Words

Draw, write or doodle in this space to represent your day

Daily Journal

Date ________________________

Location __________________

Daily Note

The best part of today was:

What I did today:

What made me smile:

Today I Felt

TODAY'S WEATHER

Today's Transportation

A Picture is Worth a Thousand Words

Draw, write or doodle in this space to represent your day

Daily Journal

Date ______________________

Location ______________________

Daily Note

The best part of today was:

What I did today:

What I am grateful for today:

Today I Felt

TODAY'S WEATHER

Today's Transportation

A Picture is Worth a Thousand Words

Draw, write or doodle in this space to represent your day

Famous Bridges of Venice

Rialto Bridge

Bridge of Sighs

Academy Bridge

Calatrava Bridge

Scalzi Bridge

Let's Build Some Bridges (hard)

1. Draw bridges (lines) between the canal banks (numbered circles).
2. The number of bridges connecting must equal the number in the circle.
3. The maximum number of bridges connecting two canal banks is two.
4. The bridges connect canal banks horizontally or vertically (not diagonally).
5. The bridges may not cross each other.
6. The bridges and canal banks must form a single connected group.

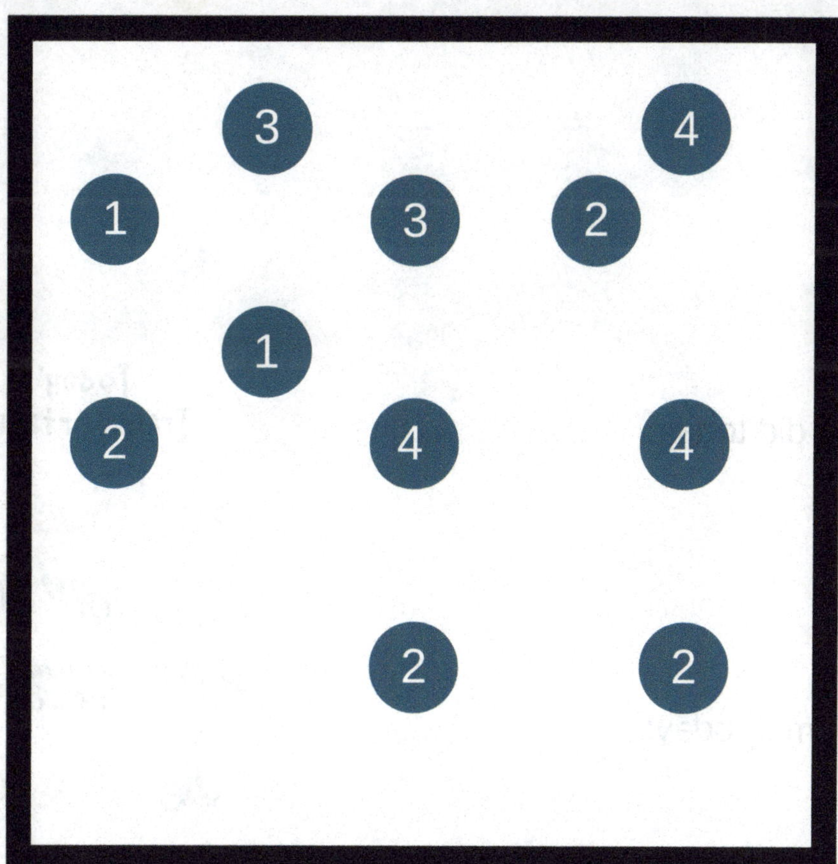

The solution is at the back of the book.

Daily Journal

Date _______________________

Location _______________________

Daily Note

The best part of today was:

What I did today:

Who I met today:

Today I Felt

TODAY'S WEATHER

Today's Transportation

A Picture is Worth a Thousand Words

Draw, write or doodle in this space to represent your day

Daily Journal

Date ___________________________

Location ___________________________

Today I Felt

Daily Note

The best part of today was:

What I did today:

Where we went today:

TODAY'S WEATHER

Today's Transportation

A Picture is Worth a Thousand Words

Draw, write or doodle in this space to represent your day

Daily Journal

Date ________________________

Location ________________________

Daily Note

The best part of today was:

What I did today:

Today I Felt

TODAY'S WEATHER

Today's Transportation

A Picture is Worth a Thousand Words

Draw, write or doodle in this space to represent your day

Spot the Differences

There are ten differences between the maps. Can you spot them all?

Spot the Differences

The solution is at the back of the book.

Daily Journal

Date ______________________

Location ______________________

Daily Note

The best part of today was:

What I did today:

Today I learned:

A Picture is Worth a Thousand Words

Draw, write or doodle in this space to represent your day

Daily Journal

Date _______________________

Location _______________________

Daily Note

The best part of today was:

What I did today:

Today was:

Busy ☐   Chill ☐

Today I Felt

TODAY'S WEATHER

Today's Transportation

A Picture is Worth a Thousand Words

Draw, write or doodle in this space to represent your day

Daily Journal

Date ________________________

Location ________________________

Daily Note

The best part of today was:

What I did today:

What made me laugh:

Today I Felt

TODAY'S WEATHER

Today's Transportation

A Picture is Worth a Thousand Words

Draw, write or doodle in this space to represent your day

The Best of Italy
In My Personal Opinion

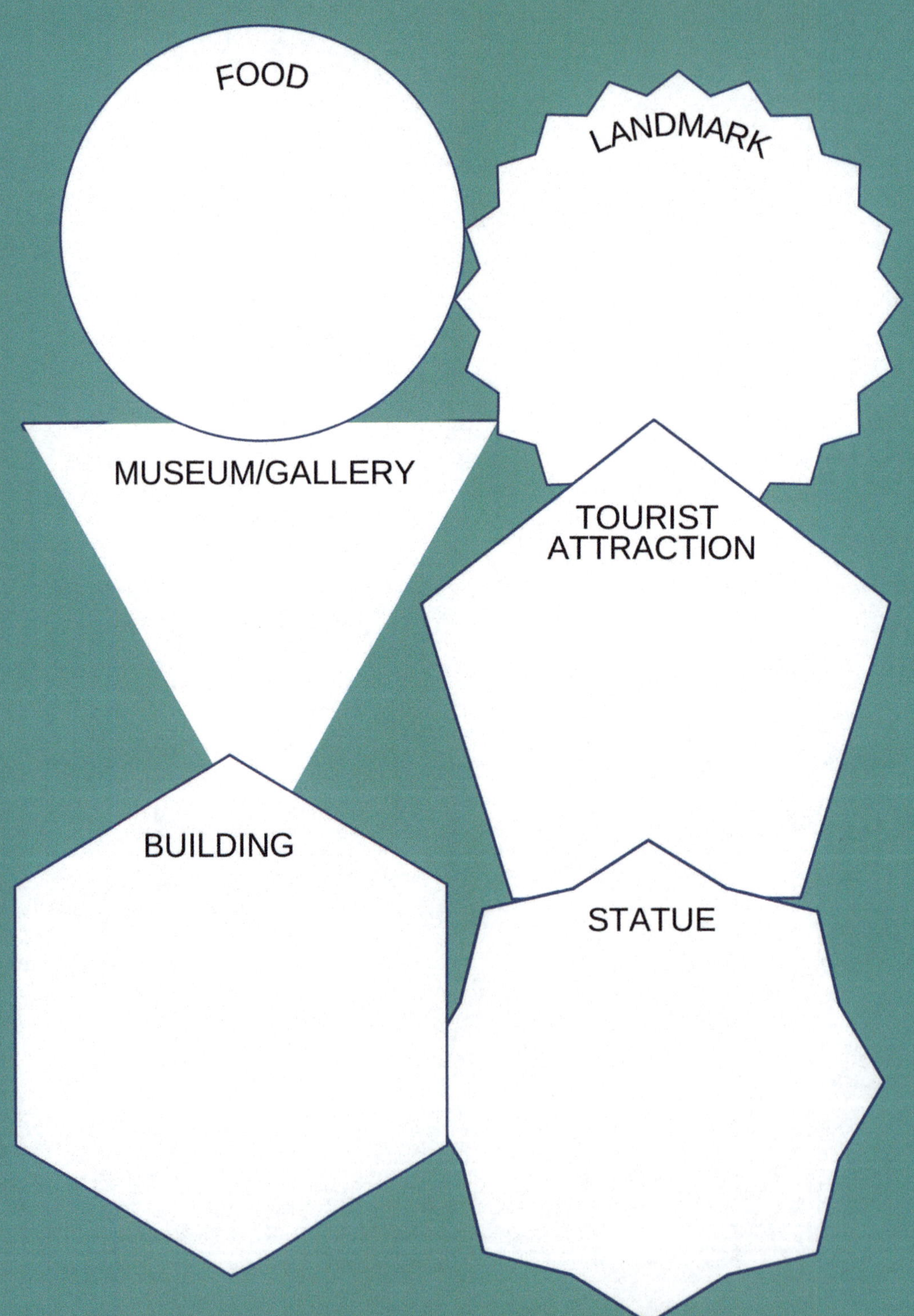

Where I Went
Color the dots for each city you visited.

Fun Fact: the most visited cities in Italy are:

1. Rome
2. Venice
3. Florence
4. Milan
5. Naples

Daily Journal

Date ___________________

Location _______________

Daily Note

The best part of today was:

What I did today:

A Picture is Worth a Thousand Words

Draw, write or doodle in this space to represent your day

Daily Journal

Date _______________________

Location _______________________

Daily Note

The best part of today was:

What I did today:

Who I met today:

Today I Felt

TODAY'S WEATHER

Today's Transportation

A Picture is Worth a Thousand Words

Draw, write or doodle in this space to represent your day

Daily Journal – Heading Home

Date _______________________

Location _______________________

Daily Note

Today we leave Italy and go home 😢

What I will miss the most about Italy:

Who I'm excited to see so I can tell them all about my trip!:

Today I Felt

TODAY'S WEATHER

Today's Transportation

A Picture is Worth a Thousand Words

Draw, write or doodle in this space to represent your day

How to Make an Envelope
For Your Small Souvenirs

What you'll need:
- scissors
- a glue stick (you can substitute with tape or staples)

Step 1: cut along the dotted lines being careful not to remove the page from the book

Step 2: fold the paper where it says "fold **up**", and make a crease.

Step 3: Unfold from step 2, and lay a thin line of glue where it says "glue".

Step 4: repeat step 2, only this time, run your finger along both sides to glue the paper shut.

Step 5: Once the glue has dried, fold the paper where it says "fold **down**" to make a flap for your envelope.

Now you have a place to keep ticket stubs, tokens, stamps, or any other tiny souvenir you pick up on your trip.

If you prefer, you can also use the pages titled "Souvenirs" to tape or glue small items.

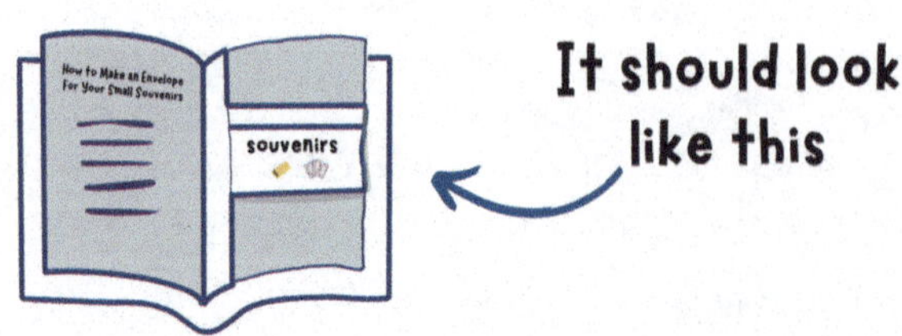

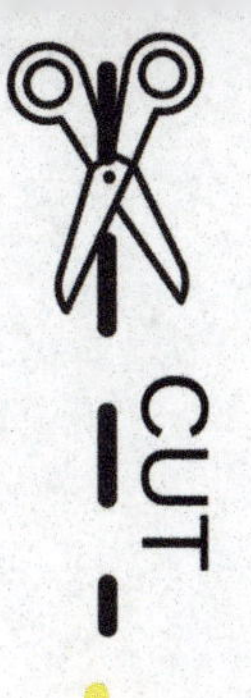

Fold Down

Fold Up

Below is printed upside down on purpose. Once you create an envelope, and fold the paper, this becomes the front of the envelope and right-side-up.

souvenirs

Airport/Train Station Bingo

It's been a great trip to Italy. But now you must sit at the airport or train station again before going home. Ready for another round of Bingo? Cross off everything you see. Can you get a straight line? How about a full card?

Souvenirs

Tape or glue paper
souvenirs on these two sheets.
Examples of paper souvenirs:

ticket stub
boarding pass
luggage tag
receipt
postcard
book mark
map
menu
program
brochure

Souvenirs

Larger items like a map can be folded first, and then just one section can be attached to the page so you can open it up.

Tape or glue under here then fold it down on top

Answers

Get to The Train Station

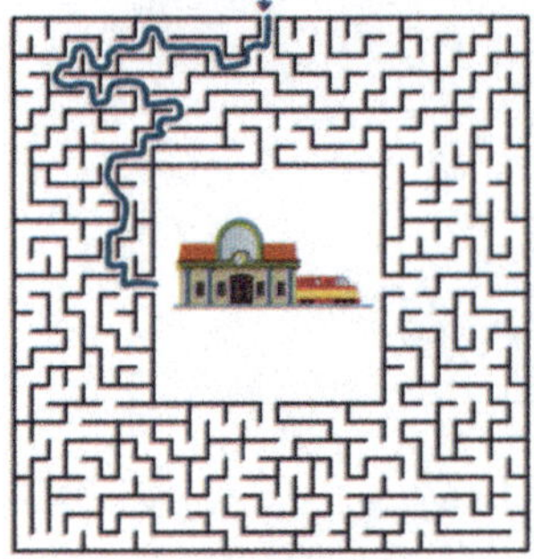

Can You Climb to the top?

Use the hypogeum to get to the arena

Italian Things Sudoku (easy)

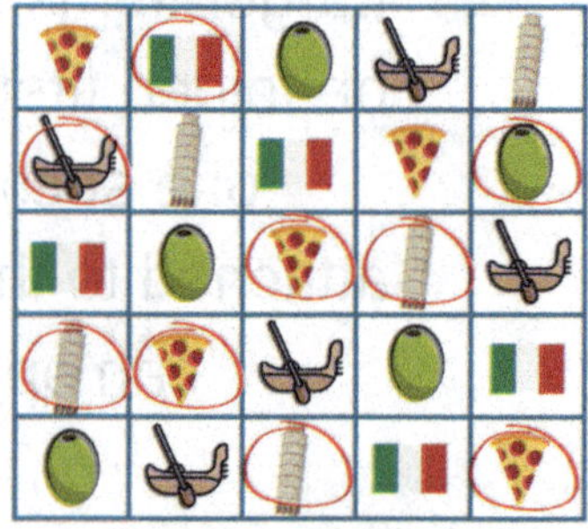

Italian Things Sudoku (medium)

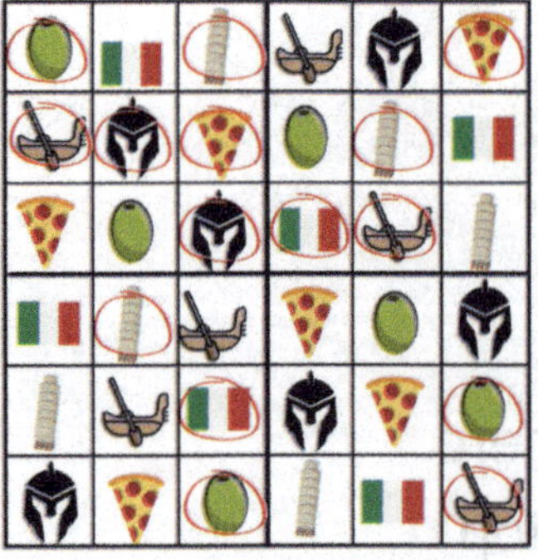

Italian Things Sudoku (hard)

Let's Build Some Bridges

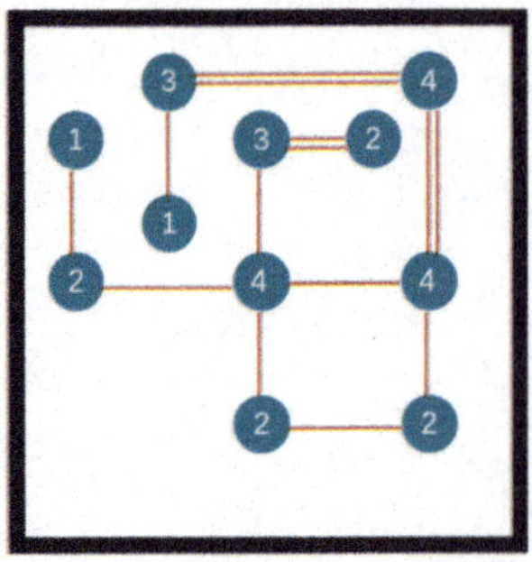

Spot the Differences

Italian Vacation – Logic Puzzle (hard)

	Rome	Venice	Naples	Pisa	7 days	10 days	14 days	21 days
Adams	✓	✗	✗	✗	✗	✗	✓	✗
Chong	✗	✗	✗	✓	✓	✗	✗	✗
Garcia	✗	✓	✗	✗	✗	✓	✗	✗
Jones	✗	✗	✓	✗	✗	✗	✗	✓
7 days	✗	✗	✗	✓				
10 days	✗	✓	✗	✗				
14 days	✓	✗	✗	✗				
21 days	✗	✗	✓	✗				

Adams visited Rome for 14 days.

Chong visited Pisa for 7 days.

Garcia visited Venice for 10 days.

Jones visited Naples for 21 days.

Clues:

1. The Adams were on vacation twice as long as the family who went to Pisa. **The only number twice as big as any other, is 14.**

2. The family that was gone for 21 days visited Naples.

3. The Jones family visited the city that invented pizza. **Pizza was invented in Naples.**

4. The Garcia family went to the city of canals for more than a week. **Venice is known as the city of canals.**

5. The Chong family went to Pisa to take a funny photo.

6. The Adams family vacationed in the capital of Italy. **Rome is the capital of Italy.**

We hope you had fun with this book and that it helped you to create a wonderful souvenir of your trip to Italy. Here's a space for you to draw a picture of your favorite memory of your trip.

Made in the USA
Coppell, TX
03 December 2024

41652502R10057